OLE & LENA JOKES — BOOK 4

by Red Stangland
"King of Scandinavian Jokes"

published by

NORSE PRESS

Box 1554
Sioux Falls, SD 57101
U.S.A.

Illustrations by
Marian Henjum

ISBN 0-0613274-8-0

First Printing

INTRODUCTION

You don't have to be Scandinavian to tell Ole & Lena jokes. Or to appreciate them. All you need to be is a person who likes to consider the funny side of life. Even sickness and calamity need a touch of humor to ease the pains and frustrations of life.

That's where Ole & Lena come in. Ole & Lena *invented* calamity, but their stoic natures override any and all problems that arise.

Red Stangland is a humorist of Norwegian heritage who has an experienced sense of what is funny, especially from the Scandinavian point of view.

Besides being a broadcaster, Red is also a stand-up comic with his side-kick, Uncle Torvald. The pair has entertained countless conventions, parties and assorted public get-togethers.

The harvest of jokes they have picked up along the way appears in this newest collection of Ole & Lena jokes that are such a delight to so many people throughout America. So, prepare to laugh. It is GOOD for you . . . AND those around you.

Ole might be considered a bit gullible. Last week, he contributed $5 to a collection being taken for the widow of the Unknown Soldier.

Ole recently spent some time in the hospital. He now laughingly refers to an enema as "a goose with a gush."

When Ole and Lena first got married, they honeymooned in California. One of their experiences was to visit the Art Linkletter radio show. To their surprise, Art Linkletter chose them to be interviewed.

Said Linkletter, "So your names are Ole and Lena and you're on your honeymoon. Are you staying here in Hollywood?"

"Oh no," answered Lena. "We have relations in the Valley."

Ole had to see a doctor, so he chose one who claimed to diagnose people simply by looking into their eyes. As he looked into Ole's eyes, he stated, "I believe you have a LOCKED BOWEL."

"Oh no," said Ole. "I got da diarrhea. So you're wrong."

"I'm never wrong," said the doctor. "You DO have a locked bowel. It just happens to be locked in the OPEN position."

Lena went to the doctor about her memory loss. The doctor made her pay in advance.

Lena was having a problem with her left ear, so she got an appointment with the ear specialist. The doctor was looking through his instrument into Lena's ear when he said: "Lena...I don't know what to think of this. I'm looking in your ear and I THINK I see a suppository in there."

"Uff Da," exclaimed Lena. "Now I remember vhat I did vid my hearing aid."

Ole was talking to Lars about the problems of growing old. Said Ole, "I heard da odder day dat dere is FOUR stages of getting older.
Stage One...is forgetting FACES.
Stage Two...is forgetting NAMES.
Stage Three...is forgetting to zip UP."
"Yah," said Lars. "Vhat is da fourth stage?"
Ole: "Forgetting to zip DOWN!"

Ole was on an airplane trip. His companion in the next seat was a gorgeous young woman who made Ole's heart skip a couple of beats.

"Where are you going?" asked the young Miss.

"Minneapolis," said Ole.

"Same here," said the gal. "I'm going to Minneapolis to meet the man of my dreams...because I read in a magazine that the sexiest, most romantic men on earth are NORWEGIANS and AMERICAN INDIANS. By the way, what is YOUR name?"

Said Ole shyly, "Ole Red Feather."

Mrs. Helga Knakkebrod was making some snide remarks about Ole, implying he was a failure. Lena indignantly came to Ole's defense, saying, "Ole started life at the bottom. It yust so happened he felt comfortable there."

4

"LENA...I DON'T KNOW WHAT TO THINK OF THIS."

Helga Rommegrot lost her husband, Knute. She was grief stricken. Then one day, an insurance man came to her door and presented Helga with a check for $50,000.

Later, Helga confided to Lena, "You know, I vould almost be villing to give $20,000 yust to have him back."

Ole's old-time friend, Hans, was visiting from Brooklyn. While Lena fixed supper, Ole confided to Hans that lately he had noticed he had developed special powers from God.

Said Ole, "Yah, ven I get up to go to da bathroom in da middle of da night, da light goes on vidout me pushing da svitch. I figger God has given me special powers."

After supper, Hans took Lena aside and asked about Ole's supposed "special powers."

Lena laughed and explained to Hans, "Don't pay any attention to dat, Hans. Since Ole has got a lttle older, in da middle of da night ven he tinks he is going to da bathroom, he's actually piddling in da refrigerator."

Ole was in an accident and landed in the hospital with a fractured leg and a broken jaw. Since the doctors had to wire his jaws shut, the problem was how to feed Ole so he wouldn't starve. So the nurses decided to feed him anally with a tube. They started out with some lukewarm chicken soup; then, for dessert, some warm cocoa. As the chocolate feeding began, Ole began screaming between his wired-together teeth.

"What's the matter, Ole?" asked one of the nurses. "Too HOT?"

"No," said Ole. "TOO SWEET."

Ole says that the way to identify a funeral procession in North Dakota is to notice if the combines have their lights on.

Ole went to the hospital to visit Sven who was in intensive care with an oxygen tube in his nose. Ole tried to talk to Sven but all he could get out of him was gasping and unintelligible talk. Finally, Ole impatiently thrust a note pad and pencil at Sven and said, "I can't understand you, Sven. Write it down."

So, Sven weakly scribbled on the pad, "Get your dang foot off my oxygen tube."

GUNDER: Ole, did I tell you about my new Grandson?
OLE: No. And I appreciate it.

Ole and Lars were golfing. On the fifth hole, they drove over a little hill toward the green. To their surprise, they found one ball in the cup and one two inches from the cup. Since they were both shooting Titleist balls, they didn't know who had the hole in one. So, they called on a nearby golfer, Bert Getz, to act as referee. Bert looked the situation over and finally inquired, "All right, which of you two Norwegians was shooting the orange ball?"

Ole says that Americans are funny: "First dey put sugar in a glass to make it sveet; den, a tvist of lemon to make it sour, gin to make it varm dem up, and ice to cool it off. Den dey say, "Here's to you," and drink it demselves."

An Edina man named Cholly Starksen needed to build an addition on his house; so he consulted Ole, who was a contractor, and asked him for a bid. Ole figured his bid at $1,200. The homeowner asked Ole to break down the figures. Ole replied, "$400 for labor, $400 for material, and $400 for me."

The man said he needed a couple more bids, so he next approached a Dane who said he could do the building for $2,400, explaining, $800 for labor, $800 for material, and $800 for me." Finally, Starksen looked up a Swede contractor named Swede Johnson who said he could get the job done for $3,600. When asked to explain, Swede replied, "Vell, dat's $1,200 for you, $1,200 for me, and $1,200 for dat dumb Norvegian with da low bid."

OLE: Vhat ever happened to da Lone Ranger's horse, Silver?
LARS: I heard dey put him to vork in a gold mine.
"Oh," said Ole with a chuckle. "Now, Silver Treads among da Gold."

Ole met his friend Pasquale on the street and they started talking about the demise of a mutual acquaintance named Teresa. "What did she die of?" inquired Ole.

"V.D.," answered Pasquale.

"V.D.?" exclaimed Ole. "Nobody dies from V.D. anymore."

Responded Pasquale, "They do if they give it to Big Tony."

Rasmus Svenson, who was considered a real Romeo, was philosophizing at the local tavern. He said, "I never thought I vould see da day vhen I had more money dan John Connelly, better morals dan Jimmy Swaggart, and more vimmen dan Rock Hudson."

Ole and his friends were teasing their friend Selmer Trogstad, who was a widower, for running around with younger women.

"It's dis vay," explained Selmer. "I'd much radder smell perfume . . . dan LINAMENT."

Ole got into a lot of trouble recently at the Minneapolis-St. Paul International airport. He was walking through the terminal when he spotted his old friend, Jack Trygstad.

Ole made his big mistake when he shouted across the terminal, "HI, JACK!"

Ole is working on a new song, "Our cow wouldn't give milk, so we sold him."

Ole's neighbor, Bjarne Heggestad, is a bachelor and one night while sipping a beer in the local tavern, a curvy young lady approached him with an intriguing offer. She said, "I'll do anything you want for $100."

"Follow me," said Bjarne. So, the gal did; and Bjarne proceeded to walk to his house on Elm Street. As they approached the house, Bjarne said, "Let's get this straight . . . you say you'll do ANYTHING I VANT FOR $100?"

"That's right," said the gal.

"OK," said Bjarne. "PAINT MY HOUSE."

Ole was golfing with his friends, Lars, Knute and Arnie. His friends noticed Ole playing with an unusual ball with a small antenna sticking out of it. He explained it was a ball that couldn't be lost because of the beeper system in it. Said Lars: "Vhere did you get it, Ole?"

Ole replied, "I FOUND it."

When Lena tried to give the phone operator her phone number on a long distance call, the operator inquired, "Do you have an area code?"

"No," said Lena. "Yust a little sinus trouble."

Ole's friend Tony tells about his uncle who came to the U.S. unable to speak English. Said Tony: "My uncle made a fortune by using just three little words: "Stick 'em up."

Ole bought a ticket for a flight to Chicago. He bought some flight insurance. On his way to the plane, he stepped on a scale which read his fortune. He became panicky when he read his fortune on a little card: "The investment you made today will pay off tomorrow."

Mrs. Sorenson had her husband's ashes in an hour glass. She commented to Lena that while he was alive, he never worked. "So, now," said Mrs. Sorenson, "he can be useful around da house as an egg timer."

Ole was filling out a questionnaire. To the question regarding church preference, Ole put down: "Red brick with white trim."

KEEPING MR. SORENSON BUSY.

Lena was in her car, stopped at a traffic light. The light turned red, green, amber, and then red again. A cop standing on the corner was heard to comment, "Lady, let me know when you see a color you like."

Ole calls up his doctor and says, "Every morning at 5 I have a B.M."

"Fine," said the doctor. "That's very healthy. What seems to be your problem?"

"Vell," said Ole. "I don't vake up 'til six."

Ole, the undertaker, was hauling a corpse to the cemetery in Duluth, Minnesota. As the hearse was slowing progressing up the steep hill, the rear door accidentally came open and the casket, which was on rollers, went careening down the hill . . . with Ole in hot pursuit. Just as the casket was heading into the door of a drugstore, Ole ran breathlessly up to the druggist, gasping, "Say, Doc . . . have you got anything that will stop this coffin?"

Ole and Lena took little Lars to church for the first time. After the services, they asked him how he liked it. "Vell," said little Lars, "Da music program was OK, but da commercial vas too long."

Ole says: "Dere vas a time ven a fool and his money were soon parted. Nowadays it happens to everyvun."

Sven was telling Ole about his cousin Torkel up in Minneapolis who had become a consultant. Ole says: "Vhat does a consultant do?"

Sven said, "Vell, it's something like my cat. He was roaming and prowling every night. So I had him neutered. He still goes out roaming and prowling . . . but now, only as a consultant."

Little Ole's Grandpa was having a little talk with Little Ole. Grandpa said, "Vell, it's a good ting ve all like different tings . . . oddervise everybody vould be after your Grandma."

Knute Hegermoe got tired of farming so he went off to sea and became a pirate. Ten years later, he was seen back home with a peg leg, a hook for a hand, and a black patch over one eye. Ole spotted him and asked what happened. "Vell," said Knute, "I have been a pirate and it's a tough life. Vun time in a battle a cannon ball shot off my leg, so I had to whittle myself a peg leg. Den, I got in a sword fight and lost my right hand and our ship's blacksmith made me a metal hook." Ole said, "Vell, vhat about da patch over your eye?" Knute explained that he had been up on the ship's poop deck taking navigational sightings when suddenly a seagull dive-bombed him with a mess square in the eye."

"But you couldn't lose an eye from THAT," said Ole.

"You can," said Knute, "if you just got a new hook on your hand."

Lena is some cook. It takes her an hour to cook minute rice.
(She once tried to open an egg with a can opener.)

13

Ole was in the Sears Roebuck store and observed a blind man come in with a seeing eye dog. Shortly the blind man started swinging the dog around his head by the dog's leash. A clerk stepped up and said to the blind man, "Can I be of help?" "Oh no," said the blind man, continuing to swing the seeing eye dog. "We're just looking around."

Ole was out with the boys one night and before he realized it, it was dawn. After considerable thought, Ole phoned home. When Lena answered, Ole shouted, "Don't pay da ransom, Lena. I've yust escaped."

Ole was working in a gas station when a lady drove up and let her dog out of the car. The dog started scratching itself furiously. Looking at Ole, the lady hastened to comment, "I got an itchy poochy."

"Sorry, Lady," said Ole, "I don't know a ting about dose Yapanese cars."

Ole and Lena invited a well-to-do Uncle for dinner. Little Ole looked him over and finally approached the old Uncle with a request. "Uncle Knute . . . vill you make a noise like a frog for me?" said Little Ole.

"Vy in da vorld do you vant me to make a noise like a frog?" exclaimed the Uncle.

"Because," said Little Ole, "Papa says ve are going to get a lot of money ven you croak!"

Ole ran into Lars on the street corner and mentioned Lars' absence from Sons of Norway in recent weeks. Lars said, "Vell, it's a long story. It all started vun night vhen Helga t'ought she heard da chickens making a racket. So, I grabbed my old shotgun 'cause I figured it must be a chicken teef trying to steal our chickens. I yust ran out of da house da vay I vas . . . vid my nightshirt and a pair of slippers. As I vas approaching da chicken house, I vas imagining a chicken teef in dere 'cause I could hear some clucking. So, I carefully started opening da chicken house door, lifted my shotgun and pulled back da hammers on my double barrel. All of a sudden, Old Rover, our dog, valked up behind me, lifted up my nightshirt AND COLD NOSED ME. To make a long story short, da gun vent off and ve been cleaning chickens for da past two veeks. And dat is vhy you haven't seen me at Sons of Norvay."

Lena stepped up to the clerk in the department store and said, "Can I try on dat dress in da vindow?"

The clerk responded, "We'd really prefer that you try it on in the dressing room."

An elderly couple consulted their doctor, telling him they thought they might have AIDS. When asked what gave them reason to think that they, both 80 years old, might have the disease, they replied, "We read that you can get it from annual sex."

Ole was at the rodeo watching his friend, Tex, bulldog a steer. When Tex got bowled over by the critter, Ole rushed over sympathetically, exclaiming, "You hurt BAD, Tex?" To which Tex replied between groans, "You ever heard of anybody hurt GOOD?"

Ole's boss had been invited to Ole and Lena's for supper. As Lena was setting the table, Ole's boss casually asked Little Ole what was being served for supper. Little Ole said, "I tink it is buzzard . . . because dis morning, Mama said to Papa, "If ve are going to have dat old buzzard for supper, it might as vell be tonight."

Lena doesn't like her neighbor, Mrs. Kjorpestad. Lena says Mrs. Kjorpestad's mother got morning sickness AFTER she was born. And she was so ugly, they diapered her FACE.

Ole and Lena's neighbor, Rasmus announced he was getting married. Rasmus was getting along in years, so Ole and Lena were somewhat surprised when Rasmus commented he intended to start another family. Ole winked at Lena and said to Rasmus, "You better take in a boarder." A few months later, Ole ran into Rasmus and asked about his new wife. "Yah, she's going to have a baby," beamed Rasmus. Said Ole, "What did you ever do about getting a boarder?" "Oh, da boarder," said Rasmus. "SHE'S PREGNANT TOO."

Lena says grocery shopping is getting to be just like a religious experience. She says, "All you see is people going up and down da aisles, and ven dey see da prices, dey all say, "O MY GOD. O MY GOD."

Ole, Lars and Knute were discussing ferocious creatures. Lars said, "Da tiger-eating alligator has got to be da meanest animal alive."

Knute held another opinion, saying, "Vell, I tink dat da alligator-eating tiger is really da meanest of any animal anywhere."

Ole spoke up, saying, "I hate to disagree, but in my opinion, da Tigergator is da meanest critter you'll find anywhere."

"Da Tigergator?" exclaimed Lars and Knute in a chorus. "Vhat in da world is a Tigergator?"

Replied Ole, "Da Tigergator has a tiger's head on one end and an alligator's head on the other."

"But . . . how does he go to the bathroom?" asked Lars.

"He doesn't," said Ole. "Dat's vhat makes him so mean."

Ole was sent to prison on a hold-up charge. The authorities were convinced Ole had some guns hidden somewhere, but they could get no information from him.

Come spring, Lena wrote and asked when she should plant potatoes. Ole wrote back, telling her to wait a bit. A couple of weeks later, Ole wrote to Lena, saying, "The guns are buried in the back yard where we used to plant potatoes." Naturally, the mail was censored, and the authorities dug up every inch of Ole's back yard. But, to no avail. Then, a couple of days, Ole wrote to Lena again: "NOW . . . plant the potatoes."

Lena says she doesn't figure Einstein was so smart. He apparently didn't know the spelling rule of "I before E except after C" and he did it TWICE in his name.

Ole comes home after a night on the town. Just as he is about to tiptoe upstairs, the cuckoo clock starts to cuckoo. It cuckooed three times. Ole thinks fast and figures he better do something or Lena might catch on to the late hour. So, he decided to cuckoo eight more times so Lena would think it was eleven o'clock.

The next morning Lena said, "Ole, ve got to do someting about dat cuckoo clock. Last night it cuckooed three times, hiccupped once, burped tvice, said "Oh Hell," den cuckooed eight more times."

Ole and Lena went to Decorah for the Nordic Fest. They wanted to leave a wake-up call but the motel clerk said they didn't have that service. However, the clerk had an alternative idea. He said, "Just drink two glasses of water before you go to sleep and I'll guarantee you'll be up before dawn."

Ole went hunting with a Czech named Janek in the north woods of Minnesota. They somehow became separated and by the time Ole retraced Janek's trail, the Czech had been attacked by two bears and eaten. Nearby observers called authorities who arrived on the scene and wondered which of the two bears had eaten the Czech. Ole advised them to slaughter the male . . . which they did. When Janek jumped out of the bear's stomach, the game warden asked Ole why he was so certain. "Becoss," said Ole, "it's yust like the old saying, 'Da Czech is in da male.'"

"OLE GETS HOME LATE."

Everybody is always telling Ole and Lena jokes. Now it's time we print Lena's favorite joke about the boy and girl mice playing hide and seek.

Says Lena, "Da little boy mouse is looking all over and singing, "When I FIND you . . . I'm gonna HUG you."

The little girl mouse sang back, "You can't FIND me."

Then the little boy mouse sang out, "Vhen I find you, I'm gonna KISS you."

The little girl mouse sang back, "You can't FIND me."

The little boy mouse then sang out, "Vhen I find you, I'm gonna make LOVE to you."

The little girl mouse responded, "I'm in the BREAD BOX."

Ole is working on a new book to be titled: "BUTCH CASSIDY . . . THE DAUGHTER HOPALONG NEVER TALKED ABOUT."

Ole was a traveling salesman and one day his car got stalled on a country road. A nearby farm house proved to be some Norwegians who invited him to stay the night. For supper, the menu included rommegrot. Although Ole was crazy about rommegrot, he restrained himself and took only two helpings. At bedtime, the farmer explained they only had one bed, so Ole would have to sleep between the farmer and his wife. About 3 in the morning, the farmer had to get up to tend to some farrowing sows. The farmer's wife tapped Ole on the shoulder and whispered, "Now's your chance." So, Ole tiptoed downstairs to the refrigerator and finished off the rommegrot!

Ole and Lena went to have a family picture taken. The photographer told Lena to look natural . . . so she posed with her hand in Ole's pocket.

Ole and Lars worked on a construction crew. One day Lars noticed that the foreman always left the project about an hour early. "Say Ole," suggested Lars. "Why don't WE take off a little early too . . . yust like the foreman." So they agreed to try it. As soon as Ole got home, he looked all over for Lena. Finally he opened the bedroom door . . . and there she was in bed with the foreman. Ole silently closed the door and tiptoed out of the house. The next day he confronted Lars. "Ve better not try anudder stunt like ve did yesterday. I almost got caught."

LARS: I heard that you had to shoot your dog, Fido. Was he mad?
OLE: Vell, he vasn't exactly pleased about it.

OLE: What did you get your wife for her birthday, Torvald?
TORVALD: A box of chocolates.
OLE: Was she surprised?
TORVALD: I'll say so . . . she vas expecting a mink coat.

Ole's friend, Torvald, says that nowadays when he feels romatic he goes to bed with TWO women. "Dat vay," he explains, "if I fall asleep, dey can talk to each odder."

Ole reports he recently had a nightmare . . . his wife and Dolly Parton were fighting over him. And his wife won.

Folks around town say that Ole has the Midas touch; everything he touches turns into a muffler.

Ole was a businessman, and one day got a request from the government to fill out a form about his employees. One question asked: "How many employees do you have broken down by sex?"

When Ole filled out the answer, he wrote: "Practically all of dem."

INGRID: Vould you like to see da ring dat Lars gave me?

LENA: It looks like a nice ring. And it must be a comfort to know dat he isn't a spend-thrift.

The judge had just awarded a divorce to Lena, who had charged non-support. He said to Ole, "I have decided to give your wife $400 a month for support."

"Vell, dat's fine, Judge," said Ole. "And vunce in a while I'll try to chip in a few bucks myself."

Ole was flying on an airliner when the plane encountered extremely turbulent conditions. A nervous old lady, expecting disaster, turned around to Ole and implored, "Please do something religious." So, Ole started a Bingo game.

Christ and Moses felt a need to go down among the people so they decided to appear in earthly form as a pair of golfers. As it happened, they got teamed up with Ole and Lars. On the fifth hole, which was 450 yards, Christ teed off with a nine iron over a water hazard. It landed considerably short, but right on the water's edge where it could be retrieved. Christ commenced walking to his ball . . . which meant he walked right ON the water. Ole's eyes popped out of his head as he exclaimed, "Who does he think he is? Jesus Christ?"

"He IS Jesus Christ," said Moses. "He THINKS he's Arnold Palmer."

Ole and Lena went for a vacation at a fancy resort in the Bahamas. There were bell boys and waiters all over the place with their hands out. That afternoon, Ole nearly drowned in the high surf because he was not used to swimming in the ocean. After the lifeguards pumped him out and got him back on his feet, Ole asked a fellow guest, "How much are you supposed to tip for sumting like dat?"

Ole and Lena's neighbor girl is quite a fast number. In fact, Lena says she was past 21 before she learned to sit up in a car.

Little Ole was late for school. He explained he had to take their registered bull to the neighbors to service a cow. The teacher asked, "Couldn't your father have done that?"

Ole replied, "Vell, maybe . . . but Pa ain't registered."

PROFESSOR: In our experiment, we put a worm in water, and another worm in a glass of whiskey. Now . . . you see, the worm in the water is healthy, active and swimming around. On the other hand, the worm in the whiskey is already dead. Now, what does that prove to you?

OLE: Vell, it proves dat if you drink vhiskey . . . you won't have vorms.

ARNIE: Say Ole, I understand you and your wife celebrated your 25th anniversary last month. I suppose you had a party . . . killed a chicken or something?

OLE: No . . . ve vouldn't do dat. I don't believe in making a chicken suffer for something dat happened 25 years ago.

Ole and Lars were talking politics. Said Ole: "Yah, dat President Bush . . . he's doing da vork of five men. Da tree Stooges . . . and Abbott and Costello."

Ole explains what happens when you cross a gorilla with a computer: "You get a Hairy Reasoner."

Ole was out of work and in looking for a job, applied at the Dingaling Brothers Cicrus. The circus manager looked Ole over from head to toe, and then disclosed that they might be able to use Ole in the Human Cannonball act. "I think you'd work out fine, Ole," said the manager. "We could use a man of your caliber."

Ole and Lena attended a Bible study course at their Lutheran Church. Pastor Arvid Nummedahl was trying to explain INVOLVEMENT and COMMITMENT.

Ole was trying to understand the concept, so he asked the Pastor, "Can you tell me da difference between INVOLVEMENT and COMMITMENT?"

"Well, Ole," said the minister. "Let me explain it to you this way. Let's say you are at a ham and egg dinner. To a chicken, that would represent INVOLVEMENT; but to the pig, it is a matter of COMMITMENT."

Ole and Lena got a parrot that used to belong to a sailor. The first thing they discovered when they got it home was that the bird swore something terrible. (He even used some words Ole had never heard befre.)

Lena decided to teach the parrot a lesson by putting him in the deep freeze. Thirty minutes later, she figured he'd probably had enough, so she opened the freezer door. There was the parrot shivering and shaking.

"Did you learn a lesson so you von't svear anymore?" demanded Lena.

"I sure as hell did," answered the parrot. "When I saw what you did to that turkey in there, I decided you meant business."

Ole had been to the doctor but had to leave for work before he could get the results. So Lena offered to find out what was what. Later that day, Lena got a call from the doctor's office instructing Ole to bring in a stool, sperm and urine sample. So Lena sent a pair of Ole's shorts.

Ole had committed the crime of murder and so was sentenced to die. The prison officials gave him a choice between eletrocution, the gas chamber, or being injected with the AIDS virus.

Ole chose the AIDS virus, so the next morning they marched him into a small room, sat him down, rolled up his sleeve and proceeded to inject the virus into his arm. When it was done, Ole commenced laughing uproariously. The warden said, "Ole, this is serious business . . . what are you laughing about?"

"Aw, dat stuff can't hurt me," laughed Ole. "I vas using a condom."

Ole had not been seen in church for quite a while. The preacher saw him on the street one day, so he asked Ole about his absence. Ole said it was because of his shabby clothes. He was ashamed to go to church. The minister was moved by the story and handed Ole a $20, telling him to get some new clothes. The following Sunday, Ole wasn't in church and when the preacher met Ole the next day, he asked him why.

"Vell, Reverend," said Ole. "Dat new suit made me look so good I decided to go down da street to da Episcopal church."

There was a doctor in Ole's community who was discovered having relations with one of his patients. The scandal forced him to leave town. Folks in the area felt that was a shame because he was the best veterinarian in the county.

KARL: Do you wake up grouchy?
OLE: No . . . I let her sleep.

A nurse in the hospital came out to the waiting room to tell Ole tat his wife had just had a baby. "I'm happy to tell you that you have a little girl," said the nurse, "but I'm sorry that I have to tell you that one foot is a bit shorter than the other."

"Vell, dat's all right," responded Ole. "Ve vere planning to call her 'Eileen' anyvay."

The teacher was writing some sentences on the blackboard when she dropped her chalk. As she bent over to pick it up, little Arnie piped up. "Teacher . . . I can see two inches above your knee." Outraged, the teacher said, "Arnie, for your impertinence, you are expelled from school for one week." Shortly, the teacher dropped the chalk again and bent over to pick it up. This time, little Ralph spoke up, "Teacher . . . I can see FOUR inches above your knee." Infuriated once again, the teacher ordered little Ralph to be expelled for TWO weeks. Ten minutes later the teacher once again dropped the chalk; and again, stooped over to pick it up. As she raised up, she noticed Little Ole grabbing his school books and heading toward the door. "Little Ole, where are you going?" asked the teacher. Answered Little Ole . . . "I'm going home, teacher, my school days are over."

Ole says he wears dark glasses around the house because it bothers him to see his Lena work so hard.

A knock at the door. Ole goes to answer it. He encounters a masked man with a gun.

"Are you a robber?" inquires Ole.

"No . . . I'm a rapist."

Ole: "Lena . . . it's for you."

Little Ole's teacher, Miss Heggebust, had announced her engagement to a local man. Her students apparently shared her joy because they brought her gifts. Little Thorleiv, whose dad owned a fruit store, brought her a box of oranges. Mary Tofteskov, whose parents ran a ladies shop, brought her a purse. Little Johnny Jensen, whose dad had a Danish bakery, brought her some delicious Danish rolls. Little Ole, whose dad, Ole, ran a liquor store, brought a box and set it on his teacher's desk. Teacher noticed something dripping from the box, and as she excitedly worked on the strings binding the box, she touched the fluid coming from the box and tasted it. "Mmmmmmmmm," said Teacher. "I'll bet your dad sent some fine French champagne or wine from his store?"

"No ma'am," said Little Ole. "Puppies."

Ole has a slogan on the bulletin board at home:
"THE HURRIER I GO, THE BEHINDER I GET."

Lena got a job writing headlines for the local paper. After one of the churches in town burned, she came up with this headline: CHURCH BURNS DOWN; HOLY SMOKE.

Lena was visiting on the front porch with her friend, Kari Roomegrot, when a delivery man brought a dozen roses. They had been sent by Ole. "How thrilling," said Kari. "I bet you're really thrilled to pieces."

Replied Lena sardonically, "Vell, all it really means is I suppose I'll have to spend da next veek or so vid my legs in midair."

"Vell," said Kari. "Vhat's da matter . . . don't you have a VASE?"

28

Ole went to the doctor for a checkup. The doctor pronounced him fit as a fiddle for a man of 75 years. "How old was your father when he died?" inquired the doctor.

"Who says he's dead?" answered Ole. "He's 95 and in terrific shape. Rides a bike and golfs every day."

"Remarkable," commented the doctor. "How old was HIS father when he died?"

"Who says he's dead?" said Ole. "He's 120 years old and really in fantastic shape. Swims every day and goes bowling. In fact, he's getting married next week."

"Why in the world would a man of 120 years of age WANT to get married?" asked the doctor.

"He doesn't WANT to," answered Ole. "He HAS to."

TORVALD: How do you recognize Ronald McDonald in a nudist camp?
LARS: By da sesame seeds on his buns.

Ole calls his dog CARPENTER because he does odd jobs around the house.

SPEAKER: In this day and age, it is hazardous to use any jokes about ethnic groups. Many politicians and other public figures have gotten into trouble by using ethnic jokes. It is much safer to tell a story using a lost civilization like the Hittities. You've read about the Hittites in the Bible. They no longer exist. So, with your permission, I would like to tell you a story about two Hittites names Ole and Lars.

Ole was lounging in front of his house when a vagrant came by and asked for a handout. Ole said, "I'll tell you what I'll do. If you go in back of da house and paint da porch, I vill give you $20." The hobo took the paint Ole handed him and a wide brush and went behind the house. About a half hour later, he reappeared, telling Ole he was finished and would like his money. Ole looked at his watch and exclaimed, "You can't get dat porch painted in yust 20 minutes."

"I sure did," said the vagrant, "and besides it's not a Porsche . . . it's a Ferrari."

Little Ole was being taught the pledge of allegiance at school. The teacher told the children to place their hand on their heart. Little Ole put HIS hand over his posterior. The teacher, amused, asked Little Ole, "Is that where your heart is?"

"It must be," answered Little Ole, "because when Grandma comes over, she pats me there and says, 'Bless your little heart.'"

Ole had gotten into the bad habit of gambling. He would gamble on horses. He would bet on football game scores. He would play cards for money. Lena was exasperated because their money was disappearing; so she made a strong appeal to Ole to cut his gambling out altogether. Ole made a promise to quit cold turkey, but Lena was skeptical. "Lena," said Ole, "I AM going to quit gambling for good. And I'll bet you ten to vun I can do it."

When Lars was courting Helga, he went to the doctor for a physical. He told the doctor he was planning to marry Helga.

The doctor said, "Lars, there's something I should tell you. Helga has got acute angina."

"Yah, I know," said Lars, grinning. "And her bosom ain't so bad either."

Lena had been feeling a bit sluggish and it was affecting her love life with Ole. She went to a doctor who prescribed a new pill that was guaranteed to put new life into Lena's urges. Lena took a pill, and according to instructions, it was to take 5 or 6 hours to take effect. Unbeknown to Lena, Ole also took one of the pills, hoping it might give him more vigor.

At 4 in the morning, Lena suddenly woke, sat upright in bed and exclaimed, "I NEED A MAN!"

Ole woke abruptly also, and HE sat up, saying: "SO DO I!"

The Petersons had just had another child. "How many is dis?" Ole asked Lena.

"This makes 10 for the Petersons," said Lena.

"Uff Da," Ole exclaimed. "Vhat are dey? Catholic or yust careless Lutherans?"

Ole and Sven sat in a tavern drinking several beers. Getting a little woozy, Sven remarked, "You know, Ole . . . you don't BUY beer . . . you yust RENT it."

Ole was appointed to a committee to deal with a snake problem in his community. So Ole sat down to write a letter to a zoo in Chicago to secure a mongoose or two. The idea was to get them to reproduce and furnish enough for the state of Wisconsin. So, Ole sat down and wrote a letter: "Please send us two Mongooses." That didn't look right, so he tore up the letter. He started the next one: "Please send us two Mongeese."

That didn't seem right either, so he tore up that letter. He finally had a better idea and wrote: "Please send us a Mongoose. And if it isn't too much trouble, send us another one, too."

Ole and Lars took off on a deer hunting trip in Northern Minnesota. The pair drove 3½ hours to the farm of a friend of Ole's near Park Rapids. It was about day-break when they arrived. Ole got out of the pickup and rang the doorbell. The farmer, Axel Swenson, answered the door and told Ole it was OK for him to hunt . . . but, as a favor, he asked Ole to shoot his faithful old mule who was sick and had to be put away. The farmer was too attached to the animal to do it himself. So, Ole said he would. When he returned to the pickup, Ole had a prankish idea. He told Lars the farmer had refused to let them hunt, so in revenge, he, Ole, was going to shoot his mule. So, Ole stepped around the barn, found the mule and put it out of its misery. Just as he shot, he heard two more shots. He turned around quickly and there was Lars waving a rifle and yelling, "I got even, too, Ole. I shot TWO OF HIS COWS!"

Little Ole and his school mate, Le Roy, had a little falling out. Said Little Ole: "My dad can lick your dad."
Le Roy: "So what? So can my Mom."

Ole was travelling up near Duluth where he spied two Finns, Toivo and Aino, fishing. And what were they using for bait? Shrimp. Ole asked WHY SHRIMP? And they answered, "Because we can't get minnows with food stamps."

Lars was trying to sing one night in the neighborhood tavern. Ole laughed and said, "Lars, you sound yust like Frank Sinatra's brother . . . Notso Hotra."

Sven said to Ole: "Better do something about your hair, Ole. It's getting thin."
Ole replied: "So what? Who want FAT hair?"

LARS: How about going bowling Thursday afternoon?

OLE: Can't. I hafta go to court.

LARS: Court? For what?

OLE: Vell, last veek Lena told me to drop my pants at the dry cleaners. So I did. My case comes up T'ursday afternoon.

Ole visited his cousin Rasmus in southern Arizona where it was extremely hot and dry. Ole remarked about the desolate surroundings.

Said Lars, "It ain't so bad . . . all it needs is water and some good people."

Ole answered, "Yah . . . da same goes for HELL."

One day Ole was mowing the lawn at home when a snooty lady drove by in her limousine. Assuming Ole was a handyman, Mrs. Gotrocks stopped her car to inquire of Ole, "My good man, could you tell me what sort of compensation you receive for mowing this yard?"

"Oh," answered Ole slyly, "vunce in a while da lady of da house lets me sleep vid her."

Ole was working in a gas station when Mrs. Sederstrom drove in with her 1969 Nash Rambler. She asked Ole, "Can I use your restroom?"

Ole misunderstood, thinking she said "Whisk broom," and answered, "Vhy don't you yust drive over to your right and I'll blow it out vid da air hose."

Ole became wealthy while living in Minneapolis. He travelled to Minneapolis to transact some business with a group of financiers. These gentlemen put Ole up at the classiest hotel, and even though Ole had grown quite old, they sent up a beautiful model to keep him company in his expensive room.

"What would you like most?" purred the young lady.

"A nice hot bath," Ole replied. So the gal ran a tub for him.

"What else?" asked the model.

"How about some thunder?" said Ole. So the gal obligingly chanted, "BOOM . . . BOOM . . . BOOM BOOM . . . BOOM BOOM."

"Great," said Ole. "Now, how about some lightning?" So the young lady switched the light on and off several times.

"Wonderful. Now, I'd like some waves," said Ole. So the gal swished her hand in the water, creating waves.

Finally, the model asked hopefully, "Ole . . . don't you want to make LOVE?"

"What?" exclaimed Ole. "In a storm like THIS?"

Knute Hegermoe lived in the country near Mt. Horeb, Wisconsin. He had a habit of riding his horse into town and then getting quite inebriated. One night, Ole and some friends decided to teach Knute a lesson; so when Knute went into the bar for a night of drinking, Ole and his friends put Knute's horse's saddle on backward. The next day, they saw Knute on the street and asked how he fared the night before.

"Oh," said Knute, "I had quite a time. Somebody played a dirty trick on me and cut da head off my horse; and I vouldn't have made it home if I hadn't stuck my finger in da horse's vind pipe."

Ole has a brother named Hans. When Hans went to Europe on vacation, he called back by trans-atlantic telephone to see how things were going at the old homestead. The first thing Ole said was: "Da cat is dead."

"Good Lord," shouted Hans. "Couldn't you break it to me gently . . . like, telling me the cat was on the roof and somehow lost its grip. Then you took it to the vet and it was very bad off for several days and finally passed away quietly. Wouldn't that have been a better way to break the news?"

Ole agreed entirely, saying, "Yah, I suppose you're right, Hans.

Hans said, "I'm glad you agree. By the way, how is Mother?"

Answered Ole, "Mother's on the roof . . ."

Ole was drinking double shots of whiskey; every so often he would pull out a picture of Lena. Lars asked what the deal was and Ole said that after drinking double whiskies for a few hours, when Lena's picture started looking good to him, he knew it was time to quit drinking and go home.

Little Ole was called on in school to recite the pledge of allegiance. This is the way Little Ole interpreted it: "I pledge allegiance to da flag and to the Republicans for Richard Stands. Vun naked individual vid liberty and yustice for all."

Ole, Lena and Lars were heading for Minneapolis. As they were going through Mankato, the old car threw a piston which ruined the motor. So they decided to just abandon the car on the street. As they walked down the road, they came to a used car lot and asked what was available. The salesman asked how much money they had . . . which turned out to be only $15. The salesman said, "Well, I can't do anything for $15 for a car. But, tell you what . . . we have a camel we took in on trade and he'll get you to Minneapolis. All you have to do is ride on his hump, and when he comes to a stop light, he'll stop. When it turns green, he'll go." So, the three decided to take it and they got aboard the camel. Sure enough, the camel stopped at the first stop sign, and started again when it turned green.

Later in the day, the car salesman spotted Ole, Lena and Lars walking down the road. No camel. When he asked about the camel, Ole explained: "Vell, ve vere doing fine for a vhile, da camel stopped and started yust like you said. Den, ve came to a stop light and a kid in a convertible vid his girlfriend pulled up alongside. He looked at us and said, "Look at those three nuts on that camel." Vell, ve got off da camel to have a look . . . and da LIGHT TURNED GREEN . . . and away went da camel."

Why are people in Stoughton, Wisconsin smarter than the people in New York? Because the people in Stoughton, Wisconsin know where New York is. But the people in New York don't know where Stoughton, Wisconsin is.

Ole saw this sign on the highway: $100 FINE FOR LITTERING. As he threw a banana peel out of his car window, Ole remarked, "That's fine with me . . . I could use the hundred dollars."

Ole and Lena's next door neighbor is Mrs. Fiskeland. Lena says the woman is so dumb that she thinks "El Salvador" is a Mexican refrigerator.

Lena called her friend Ingeborg for their daily chat. She remarked how Ole had acquired a new habit of taking his rod and reel and fishing in the toilet.

"Why don't you take him to the doctor?" queried Ingeborg.

"Don't have time," said Lena. "I'm too busy cleaning fish."

Ole came home from a PTA meeting and told Lena how the school system planned to economize.

"Dey are going to have SEX EDUCATION and DRIVERS EDUCATION . . . use da SAME CAR," explained Ole.

Ole chopped wood for five hours for the Lutheran preacher. When he finished, he rang the doorbell at the parsonage so he could be paid. The preacher, seeking a bit of sympathy, said, "I hope you don't charge a lot, Ole . . . you see, I am just a poor preacher."

"Yah, I know," said Ole. "I've heard you preach."

Lena called the airlines information desk and inquired, "How long does it take to fly from Minnneapolis to Fargo?"

"Just a minute," said the busy clerk.

"Vell," said Lena, "if it has to go dat fast, I tink I'll yust take da bus."

OLE GOES FISHING.

Ole and Sven were drinking beer in the tavern when suddenly the fire alarm sounded across the street. All the volunteer firemen got up from their stools and left. When Sven started to go, Ole said, "Sven, I didn't know you vas a volunteer fireman."

"I'm not," answered Sven. "But my girlfriend's husband IS."

Ole met Lars on the street. "What's new, Lars?" asked Ole.

"My vife yust ran off vid my best friend."

"Your best friend?" exclaimed Ole. "I thought *I* vas your best friend."

"You vas," admitted Lars, "until dis guy ran off vid my vife."

LENA: Ole, I am to be in da amateur theatrical. Vhat vould folks say if I vas to vear tights?
OLE: Dey vould probably say I married you for your money.

Ole helped a nun across the street during the rush hour. When they got across safely, the nun thanked Ole profusely. "Dat's OK," said Ole, "any friend of Zorro is a friend of mine."

Little Ole was given an assignment in Sunday school class to draw a Christmas picture of the Christ Child and his family fleeing for Egypt. Little Ole made a crayon drawing showing the holy family on a jet plane. Ole's Sunday school teacher, Mrs. Nearman was amused and asked little Ole how the Christ child and family could have gone to Egypt by plane. Little Ole had an explanation. "Dey ver taken dere by Pontius da Pilot."

Ole rushed home with good news. "Lena . . . I yust found a great yob . . . good salary . . . free health and life insurance, and plenty of coffee breaks."

"Wonderful," exclaimed Lena. "I'm proud of you. Vhen does it start?"

Ole responded, "You start Monday morning."

Lena says, "My doctor doesn't believe in acupuncture. He voud radder stick you vid his bill."

Ole bought a farm near Frost, Minnesota. He started out with two windmills, but shortly took one of them down, explaining, "I figger dere ain't enough vind for TWO of dem."

Ole and Lena took a trip to California. When they came to the town of San Jose, Ole looked at the "Welcome to San Jose" sign and asked Lena how the name of the town was pronounced: "Is it San Ho-zee, San Ho-zay, San Jo-zee . . . or WHAT?"

"I yust don't know," said Lena. "Let's stop in at this restaurant and have a cup of coffee and we'll find out."

So, they stopped the car and parked and went in for coffee. As they were being served, Ole asked the waitress, "Say, Miss, how do you say da name of dis place?"

Said the waitress, very distinctly, "D A I R Y Q U E E N."

Ole says, "Prices are getting so high dat da only vuns dat can make a deposit on a new car are da PIGEONS."

Ole and Lena had a nice little mixed breed dog. For the first three years of his life, the dog thought his name was "Down boy!"

Ole's favorite drinking toast: "Vhatever you vish for me, I vish YOU double."

Ole and Lena were expecting their first child. The doctor came to their little house which unfortunately didn't have electric lights. So, while the doctor prepared Lena for delivery, he had Ole hold the lantern. Suddenly the doctor announced, "Ole, you and Lena have a little BOY!"

"Svell," said Ole. "I tink I'll go to da tavern and have a drink vid da boys to celebrate."

"Wait a minute Ole," said the doctor. "Here comes ANOTHER ONE! It's a GIRL!"

"Vunderful," said Ole. "Now I can go down for a beer."

"No . . . dont' go yet, Ole," said the doc. "Hold up that lantern again. Here comes ANOTHER ONE!"

"Say, Doc," exclaimed Ole, "do you suppose it's da LIGHT dat's attracting dem?"

Lena was bemoaning her family's poor economic status. Said Lena, "Elvis Presley cleared $15 million last year. And here Ole is alive and he can't even get a JOB!"

Ole met a guy the other day who is half Norwegian and half Palestinian Arab.

His name? "Yasser Yubetcha."

" DO YOU SUPPOSE IT'S DA LIGHT
DAT'S ATTRACTING DEM?"

Ole took a trip to Russia, and while in Russia was surprised to be hosted by the head Red himself, Mikhail Gorbachev. Gorby was showing Ole around Red Square in a big Russian limousine. Suddenly, Ole witnessed a Russian soldier shooting a civilian. Ole said, "Mr. Gorbachev . . . I thought you had "glasnost" over here and now I see you shooting people." Gorbachev said he was surprised, too, so he had the chauffeur drive over to the soldier to ask the reason for his act.

"You see, Comrade Gorbachev," said the soldier, "it is on account of the curfew."

"The curfew?" snorted Gorbachev. "The curfew isn't until 10 p.m. and here it is only 9."

"I know, Comrade Gorbachev," said the soldier. "But this man comes from my neighborhood and I know he couldn't possibly have made it home in only an hour."

Ole went into Norm Blomborg's barber shop for a haircut. An acquaintance (a Swede) named Karl Blomquist sat in the next chair to have his hair cut too. Blomquist's barber finished first; he then asked Karl if he wanted some fancy hair tonic put on. But Blomquist declined, saying, "My wife always says that stuff makes me smell like I've been to a French bordello." When Ole's barber finished with him, he asked Ole if HE wanted some of the fancy hair tonic.

"Yah, go ahead. My Lena doesn't know what a French bordello smells like."

LARS: My cousin Hugo has put together a funny car. He took da bumper from a '68 Chevy, he took da engine from a '72 Ford. Den he took da body and transmission from a '69 Buick.
OLE: Vhat did he get?
LARS: Four years vid time off for good behavior.

An oil drilling company in Texas had a big well fire. Even Red Adair couldn't put it out. They offered a reward of $50,000. A Norwegian fire department from Southern Texas offered to come up to try to put out the fire. As they came roaring up the highway, they turned off into the oil field . . . not only UP to the oil fire, but right IN it. The Norwegian firemen jumped out of their fire truck and began thrashing the fire with their jackets. Miraculously, the fire was put out by these Norwegians! As the superintendent reacted with amazement, he led Ole, the fire chief, into the company office where he made out a check for $50,000. "Congratulations, Ole," he said. "Here's your $50,000. Now, what do you plan to do with the money?"

"Vell," said Ole, "first of all ve vill haff to get da brakes fixed on our fire truck."

> Ole says that Lena is on a banana diet. "She hasn't lost any weight," reports Ole . . . "but you should see her climb trees."

OLE: What do you get when you mix holy water and prune juice?
KNUTE: Vell, I tink you get a religious movement.

> Lena went downtown to buy a single shoe to send to her son who was in the army. (He'd written home that he'd grown another foot.)

Ole is quite a clown . . . always joking. Even in the hospital. When he was laid up in the hospital and someone knocked at the door, he'd call out, "Who goes dere . . . friend or enema?"

A DOG NAMED SEX
(Written by Ole)

For protection, my father got me a German Shepherd dog. Ven he found out I vas Norvegian, da dog bit me. He vas a vonderful vatch dog. Vun night vhile I was being held up by a robber, da dog vatched.

Most people who have dogs call dem Rover or Spot. I called my dog "Sex." As I later found out, Sex is an embarrassing name. Vun day I took Sex for a valk and he ran away from me. I spent hours looking for da dog. A cop came over and asked me, "What are you doing in the alley at 4 in the morning?" I replied, "Looking for Sex." My case comes up Thursday.

Vun day I vent to City Hall to get a dog license, and told the clerk, "I vould like a license for Sex." He said, "I would like one too." So, I said, "But dis is a dog." And he said, "I don't care how she looks." So I said, "You don't understand; I've had Sex since I vas two years old." He said, "You must have been a very strong baby."

I told him dat vhen my vife and I separated, ve vent to court to fight for custody of da dog. I said, "Your Honor, I had Sex before I vas married." And he said, "Me too."

Den I told him dat after I got married, Sex left me; he said, "Me too." Vhen I told him dat vun time I had Sex on TV, he said, "Show off!" I told him it vas a contest. He said, "You should have sold tickets."

I also told da judge about da time vhen my vife and I vere on our honeymoon and ve took along da dog. I told da clerk dat I vanted a room to sleep in and anodder room for Sex. Da clerk said dat every room in da motel vas for Sex.

Den, I said, "You don't understand. Sex keeps me awake at night." And da clerk said, "Me too."

I give up!

There's even MORE fun waiting when you order from the book list below.

Complete list of books by Red Stangland

	Price	Qty.	Total
*Polish Jokes	$2.50		
*Norwegian Jokes	$2.50		
*Son of Norwegian Jokes	$2.50		
*Swedish Book of Knowledge	$1.50		
*Uff Da Jokes	$2.50		
*More Uff Da Jokes	$2.50		
*Ole & Lena Jokes	$2.50		
*More Ole & Lena Jokes	$2.50		
*Ole & Lena Jokes III	$2.50		
*Ole & Lena Jokes 4	$2.50		
*Yankee Jokes	$2.50		
*Office Jokes (R Rated)	$2.50		
*Norwegian Book of Knowledge	$1.50		
*O Lutefisk (nostalgia. . .growing up during the Depression in a small town)	$8.95		
*How to Become Your Own Boss . . .Shortcuts on becoming self-employed	$4.95		
	GRAND TOTAL		

ALL PRICES INCLUDE POSTAGE AND HANDLING
10% DISCOUNT ON ORDERS OVER $15.00

Name _____

Address _____

Send cash, check or mail order to:
  NORSE PRESS, Box 1554, Sioux Falls, SD 57101

A free, complete catalogue will be sent to you.